Newton Stop!

A Great Cat, but not always a Good Cat

Quinta Scott

Note to Reader: It's OK to color in this book.

For Sosie Tirzah Sia Scott,
Who corrects my spelling.

Newton Stop! is a great cat.

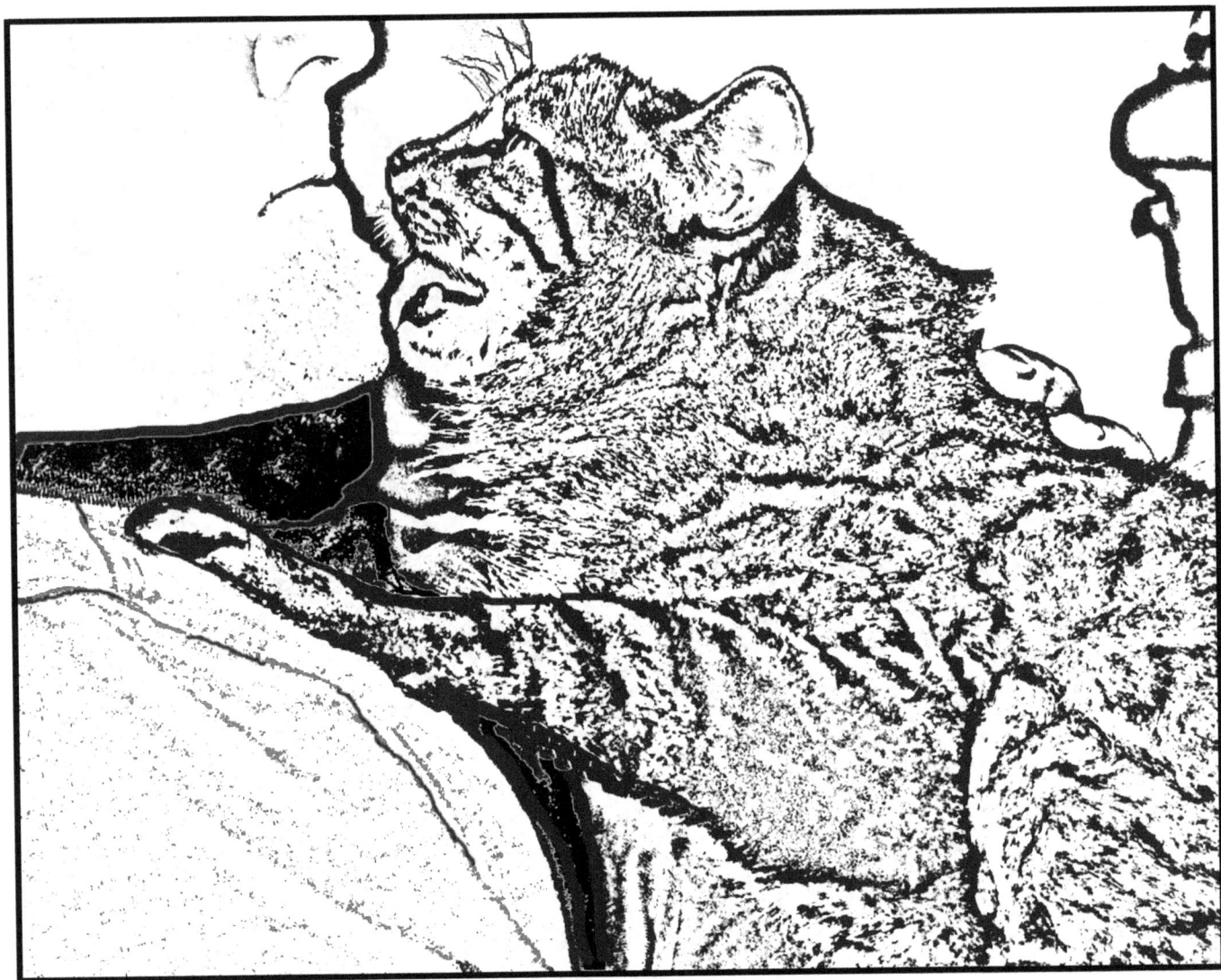

He gives rough, wet smooches.

And snoozes on his human's desk.

And grooms his buddy, Chooka.

Newton Stop! is a great cat,

but not always a good cat.

He is a bundle of bad behaviors.

He poops in inappropriate places!

Behind the boob tube.

Under the bed.

Newton, why not the catbox?
Have you no shame?

To which he replies:

Without a doubt,
this house is my domain!

Newton, I chide:

Off the dinner table!

To which he replies:

When in doubt, hide!

Boy oh boy!

Paper is his favorite toy.

He dumps the pail

to trash junk mail!

And rips and chews the daily news.

Newton Stop! I implore.

To which he replies:

When in doubt, ignore!

He scratches
the green chair to stretch.

Newton Stop! I kvetch.

To which he replies:

When in doubt, glare!

He scratches
the white chair to get out.

Newton Stop!

To which he replies:

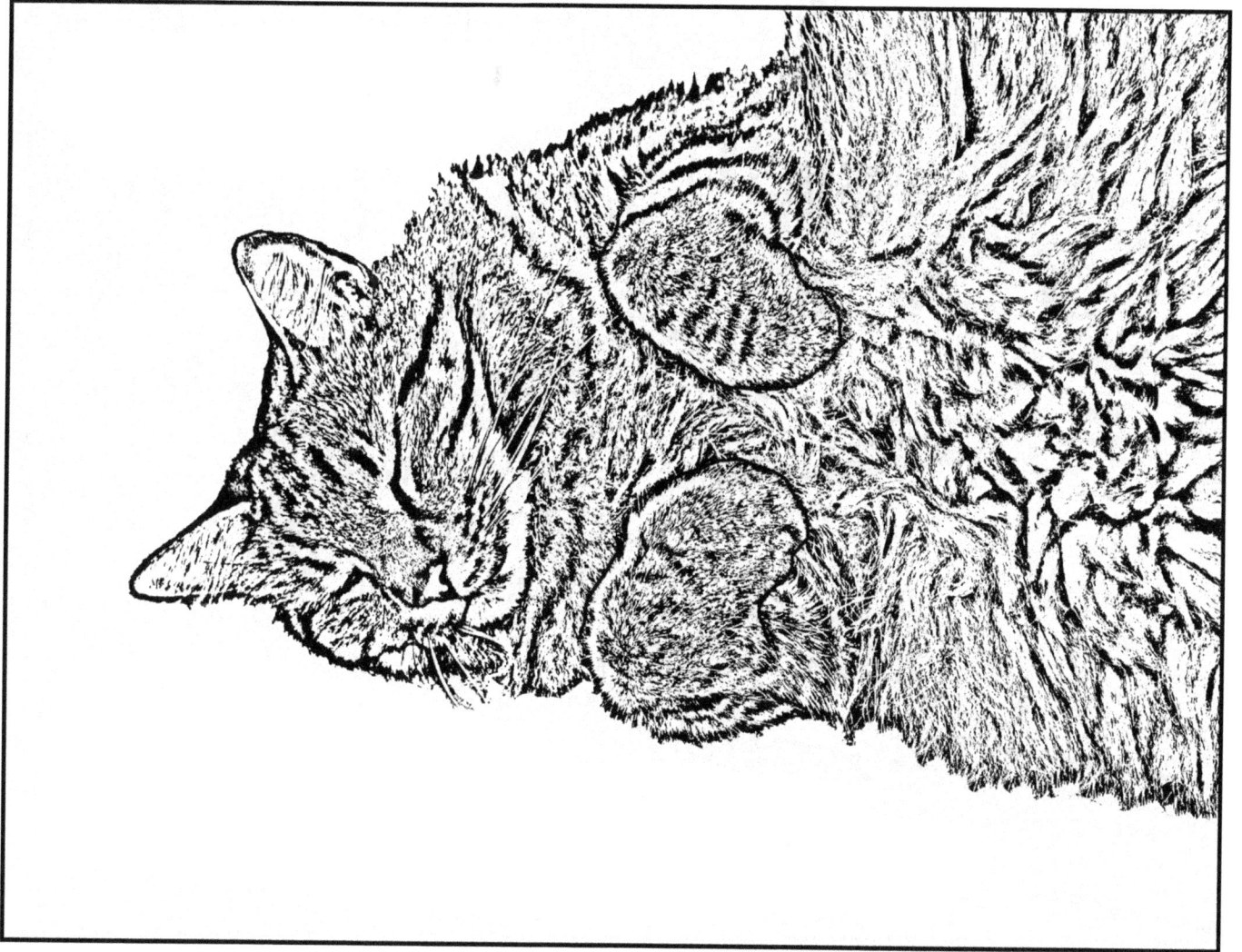

When in doubt, flop!

He scratches
the screen door to get in.

Newton Stop!

To which he replies:

When in doubt, scratch and
scratch and scratch some more!

Fight with Chooka?
Newton Stop!

On that I put the kibosh.

To which he replies:

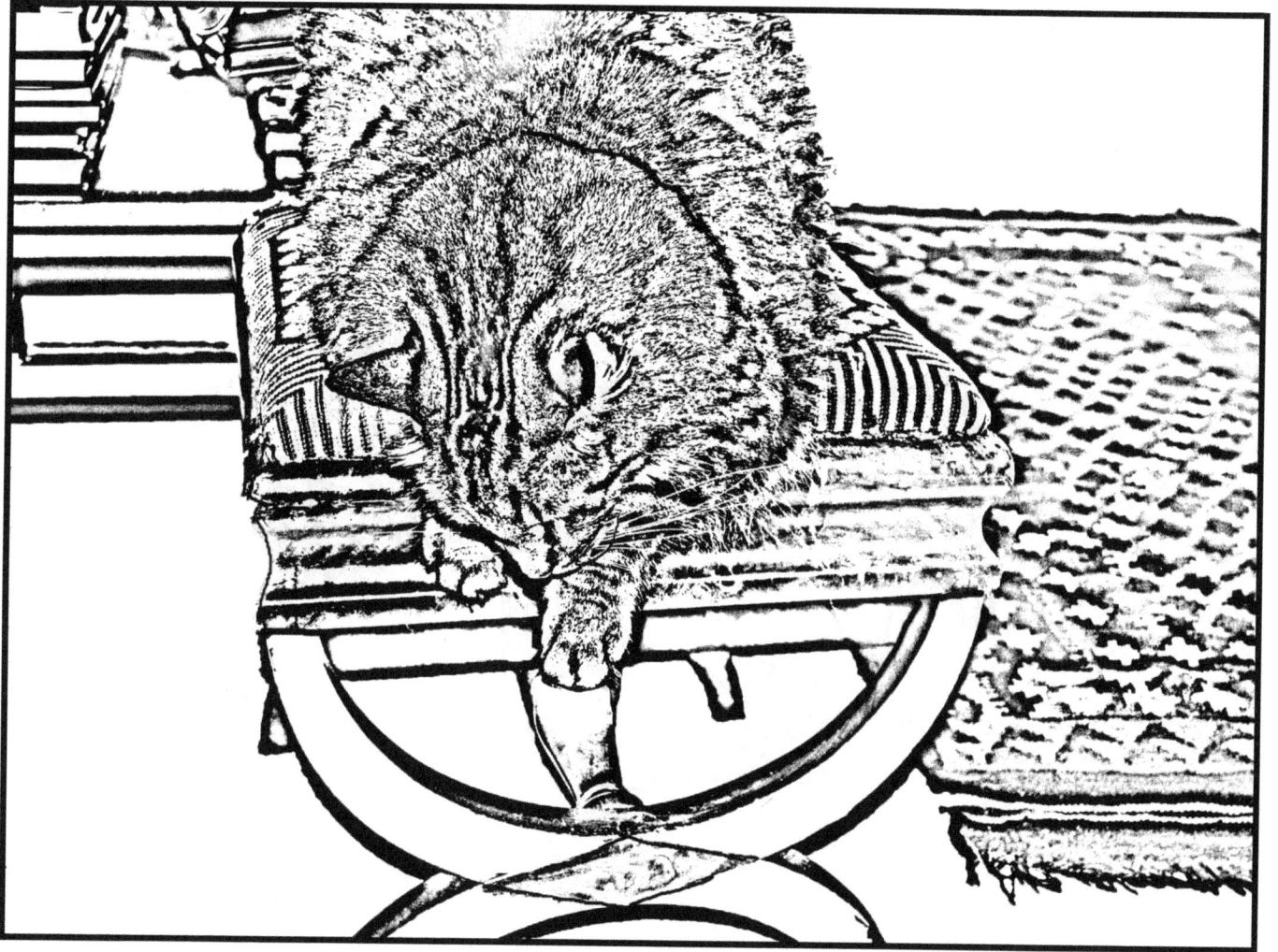

When in doubt, wash!

Even with the scratching,
and ripping,
and tearing,
and chewing,
and pooping in inappropriate places

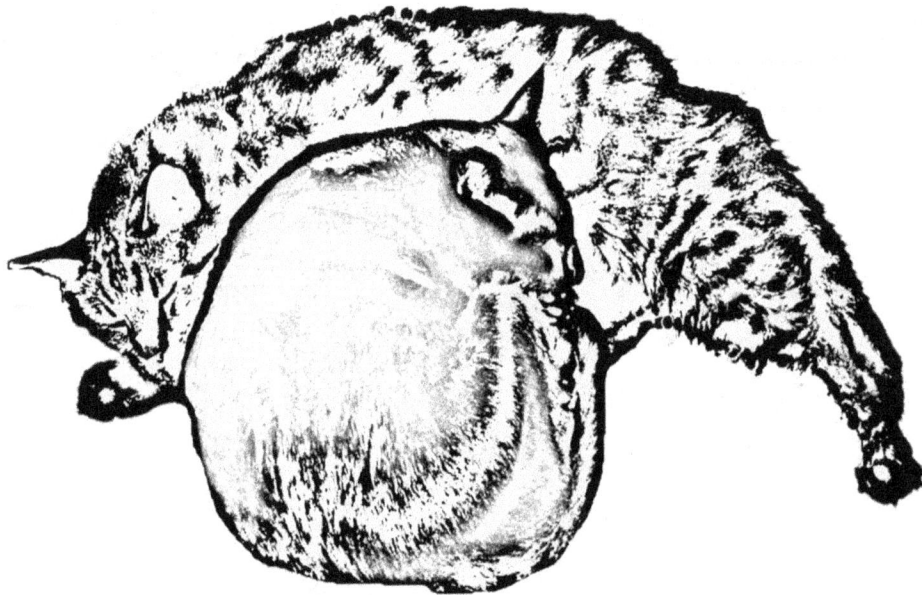

without a doubt:

Newton Stop!

is a great cat! So....

When I find him draped on the kitchen sink,

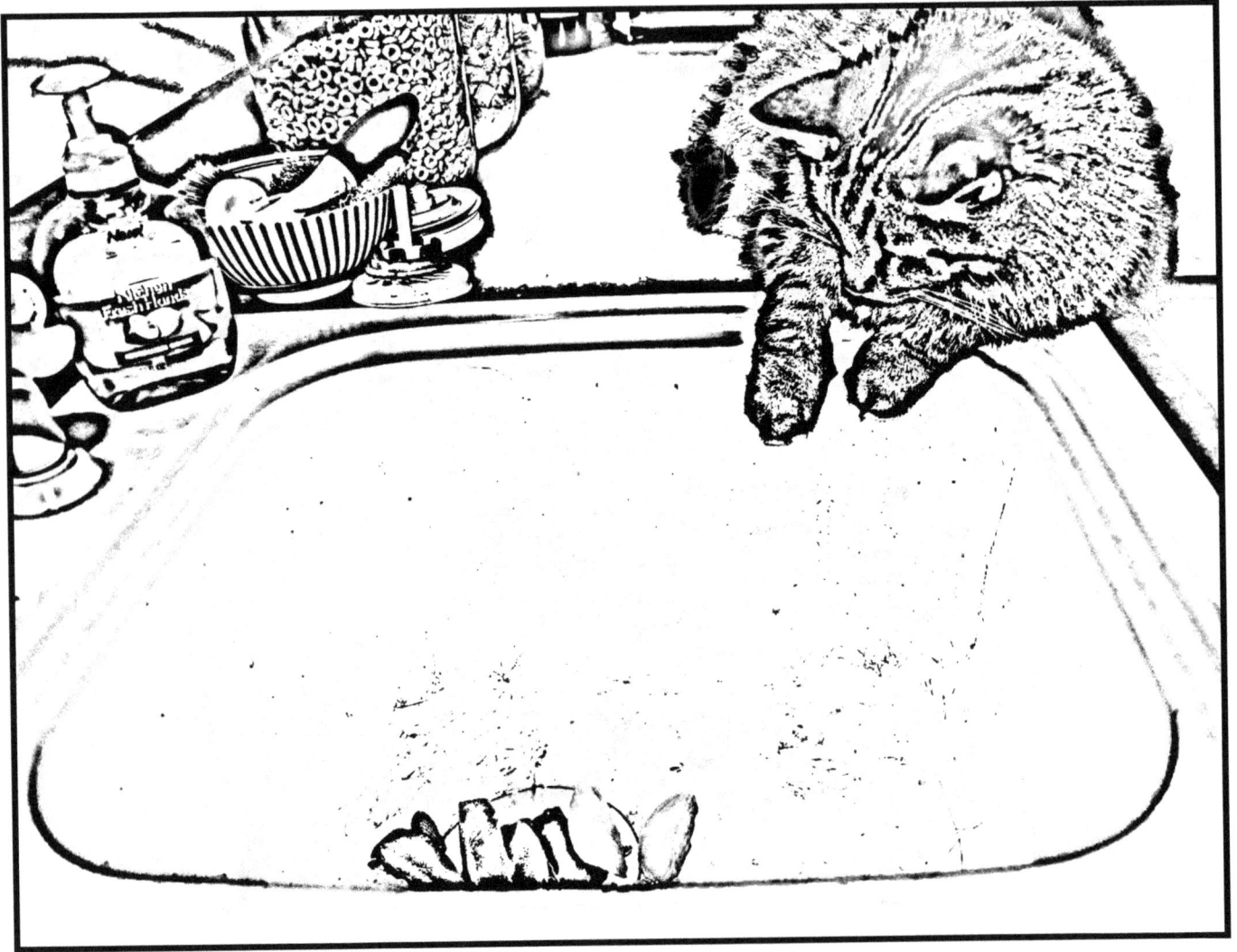

watching ice melt.

Do I belt: Newton Stop?
Do I shout: Newton Out?

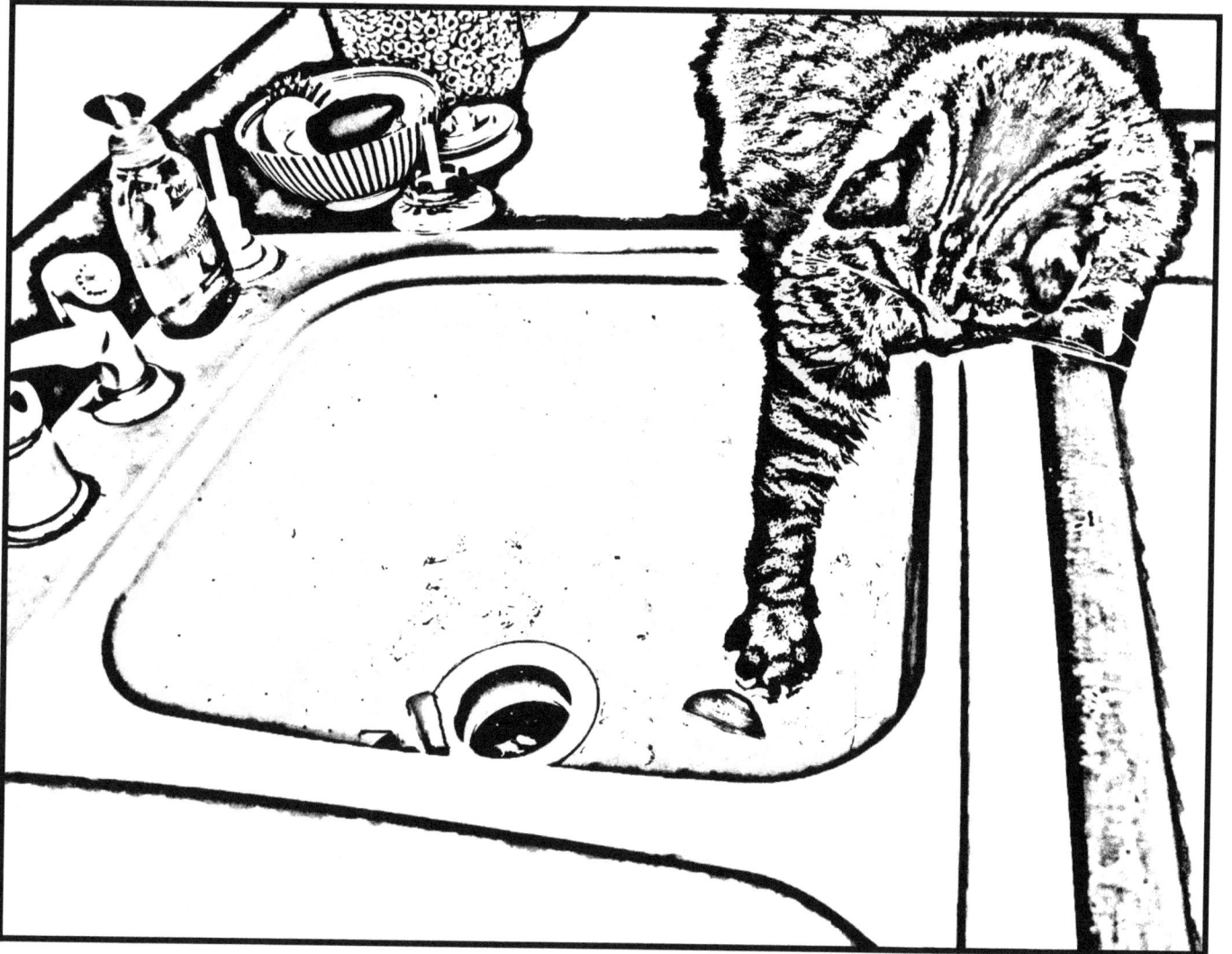

No! Instead, I coo:
Newton, I Love You!

Who Helped:

Nobody does a book alone, particularly a first book. The librarians: My friends at the Waterloo Library helped early and often: Sue Oerter criticized the first images and pointed me in the right direction. Tammi Eschmann, the children's librarian, dragged out every cat book in her collection, read an interim draft, invited me to come to Family Bedtime Story Night, and read the book to the children. Ellen Steingrubey, the director, noted images that needed to be beefed up. My teacher friends: Dottie Barbeau--Newton's sitter, who figured out how to stop him from pooping behind the TV--read the first draft and checked it for grammar, punctuation, and the typos that I just don't see. Judi Tomlinson advised me to stick with black and white images. Fanny Sue Schellhardt recommended that I show *Newton Stop!* to Marian Maag, who helped me finalize the manuscript. Other friends: Elizabeth Wright, a book designer, helped me with the graphics and the ins and outs of Photoshop. Michael Sue Schmidt came to the reading and helped me work things out after. Dorothy Uebelein, brought her grandson, Max, who asked very smart questions and insisted on meeting Newton Stop! My many, many cat-loving friends read it, laughed, and gave Newton Stop! and me pats on the head. My spouse: Barrie Scott read repeated drafts and let me know when the text got wooden and boring. My granddaughter: Sosie Tirzah Sia read a draft and corrected my spelling. Finally, everybody reassured me that "poop" is an okay word to use in a children's book--especially, the four-year-olds.

www.ingramcontent.com/pod-product-compliance
Lightning Source LLC
Chambersburg PA
CBHW081154040426
42445CB00015B/1888